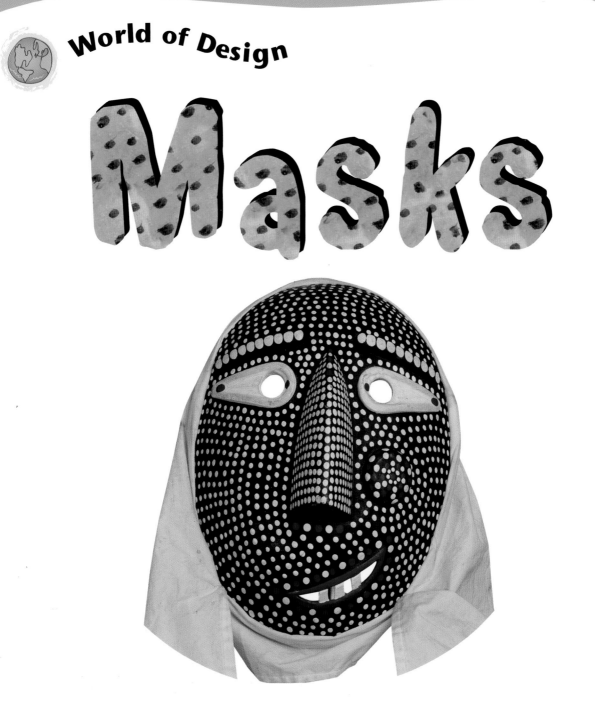

World of Design

Masks

Ruth Thomson

Photography by Neil Thomson

SEA-TO-SEA
Mankato Collingwood London

This edition first published in 2010 by
Sea-to-Sea Publications
Distributed by Black Rabbit Books
P.O. Box 3263
Mankato, Minnesota 56002

Printed in USA

9 8 7 6 5 4 3 2

Published by arrangement with the Watts
Publishing Group Ltd., London.

Library of Congress Cataloging-in-Publication Data

Thomson, Ruth, 1949-
  Masks / Ruth Thomson ; photography by Neil Thomson.
    p. cm. -- (World of design)
  Includes bibliographical references and index.
  ISBN 978-1-59771-211-8 (hardcover : alk. paper)
  1. Mask making--Juvenile literature. I. Thomson, Neil, 1948
Aug. 8- II. Title.
   TT898.T56 2010
   646.4'78--dc22
                                            2008043867
Design: Rachel Hamdi and Holly Fulbrook
Editor: Anne Civardi

The author would like to thank Kate Thackera for making the
wolf and monster masks, Louis Flynn, Lily Flynn, and Oliver
Binks for modeling the masks and Islington Education Library
Service (www.objectlessons.org) for the loan of items from
their collection.

Contents

☼ *Painted wooden cat mask from Bali*

☼ *Barkcloth and plant fiber mask from Zambia*

Mask making

All around the world people wear masks—sometimes for religious reasons, sometimes for plays or festivals and sometimes, like you, just for fun.

Masks can be made of almost any material, including wood, barkcloth, leather, clay, paper, plant fibers, stone, ivory, or metal.

☼ *Wooden Maori mask with abalone shell eyes from New Zealand*

☼ *Clay mask from Mexico*

Mexican coconut masks, decorated with painted plaster, coconut fiber, and string

A mask is usually a head or face—either of a human, animal, or bird, an imaginary creature or a powerful spirit. This book will help you understand how mask makers design and create their striking effects.

It will also show you how to make your own masks, using ones from different parts of the world as inspiration.

Skeleton papier-mâché mask from Mexico

Cat papier-mâché mask from India

Carnival mask from Cuba, made from paper pulp and cardboard

5

Creating characters

When people hide their face with a mask, they take on a new character, who has distinct features and an expression that never changes.

A mask can show:

- the age of a person —young or old
- what a character looks like—lovely or ugly, kind, cruel, or funny
- how a character is feeling—happy, sad, angry, or frightened
- a real or imaginary person.

The twisted nose and mouth, cross-eyed gaze, huge, bushy eyebrows, and large black warts make this Mexican mask look ugly and comical at the same time.

Look closer

Compare the heads of these two characters.

- They both have head-dresses, giving a clue about *who* they are.
- The close-set features of the wooden face make it look angry.
- The wide eyes, rosy cheeks, and smiling mouth of the painted king give him a cheerful, jolly look.

☀ *The deep gouges of the frown lines and eyes make the Thai wooden mask (left) far more expressive than the painted Mexican mask (right).*

Look closer

The wood carver has exaggerated the grin of this laughing mask by:

- making the eyes very narrow
- bulging out the cheeks
- making the eyebrows meet in the middle
- flaring the nostrils.

☀ *The lower jaw of this wooden Korean mask has been carved separately. It is attached by strings, so the mouth can move.*

Making character masks

1 Mark out eyes, a nose, and a mouth on a paper plate (see page 30).

2 Cut out the eye-holes and mouth. Cut a flap for the nose (see page 30).

king

girl

mermaid

pirate

3 Decide what character you want to create and cut into the edges of the plate to make hair, a crown, a beard, or a headdress.

4 Paint the face. Outline the eyes and mouth in black to make them stand out. Add extra details, such as scars, frown lines, a mustache, sequin or star jewels, or hair.

5 Attach a piece of elastic to the mask (see page 30) to hold it on your head.

Carnival masks

Once a year, many European, Latin American, and Caribbean countries celebrate Carnival. People dance through the streets wearing costumes and masks.

☼ This is the mask of Pulchinello, one of the half-masked characters in the Italian comic plays, known as Commedia dell'arte. Some European Carnival masks probably developed from this tradition.

Look closer

- The combination of sparkly sequins, soft, stripy feathers, gold trimming, and a glowing, fake jewel make this mask look very luxurious.

☼ In the past, people had fun wearing masks to a masked ball or party, called a masquerade. The masks covered half the face and were often held on a stick. People sometimes wear eye masks like this at Carnival.

Compare the cat mask on the right with the one below it.

- Both mask makers have drawn attention to the cats' ears, eyes, and noses to emphasize their sharp hearing, sight, and sense of smell.

The shiny, metal touches and stiff, plastic whiskers stand out on this Italian furry, black-cat eye mask.

Look closer

- The clashing reds and greens and touches of black make the mask below look scary.

Even though these two Cuban carnival masks are exactly the same shape, their colors and their paper pulp noses, mouths, and eyebrows give each one a very different character.

11

Making an eye mask

1 Fold a letter-sized piece of paper in half. Draw half a mask, with the nose bridge on the fold.

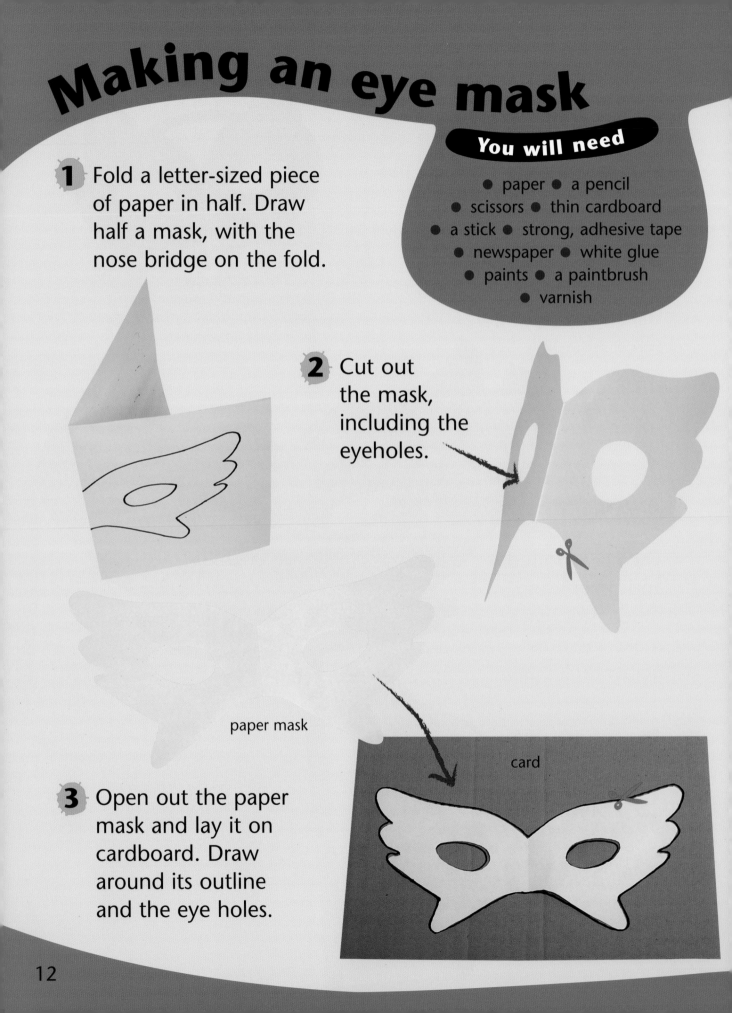

You will need

- paper ● a pencil
- scissors ● thin cardboard
- a stick ● strong, adhesive tape
- newspaper ● white glue
- paints ● a paintbrush
- varnish

2 Cut out the mask, including the eyeholes.

paper mask

card

3 Open out the paper mask and lay it on cardboard. Draw around its outline and the eye holes.

cardboard
mask

4 Cut out the
cardboard mask.

5 Tape a stick to the cardboard
mask. Cover both sides of the
mask and the stick with
papier-mâché (see page 31).
Leave the mask to dry.

*Tip: You might like to build
up some parts of the mask,
such as the eyebrows.*

6 Paint the mask and
the stick in bright
colors and patterns.
When the paint is dry,
add a coat of varnish.

Wild and woolly

Masks of wild animals are often not totally realistic. Instead, they highlight how fierce these animals really are.

Look closer

- The red ears, nostrils, and open mouth emphasize the wolf's sharp senses, as well as its dangerous nature.

- The painted black spikes framing its face suggest the wolf's shaggy fur.

- The black outlines around the eyes, nose, and mouth help these features stand out.

To create this Mexican wolf mask, the mask maker first made a clay or plaster mold of a wolf's head. Then papier-mâché was laid over the mold and left to dry. Mask makers can make many masks using the same mold.

14

- The eyes, nose, and mouth of this lion have been heavily framed to make them look much bigger.

- The strong black eyebrows draw attention to the eyes.

This painted wooden lion mask comes from Bali, an island in Indonesia, where people believe that some masks have magical powers.

In parts of India, dancers cover their body with yellow and black stripes, wear a tiger mask and tail, and perform a popular tiger-play in the open air.

Look closer

- The tiger's big eyes, ears, and nostrils make it look very fierce.

- The large red muzzle is a powerful reminder that tigers can be man-eaters.

- Black stripes help to define the tiger's ears and eyes, as well as showing its markings.

Making a wolf mask

You will need

- paper • thin cardboard
- a felt-tip pen • scissors
- paints and a paintbrush
- newspaper • white glue
- adhesive tape

The head

1 Fold a letter-sized sheet of paper in half widthways. Draw a wolf's head on one side, with the top of its head along the fold.

Do not cut along this fold.

2 Cut along the lines to make two heads, joined at the fold.

The ears

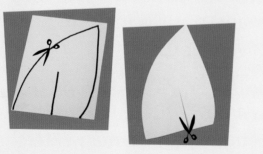

3 Fold a piece of paper in half. Draw an ear on the top half. Cut out two ears. Cut a slit in the center of both ears.

Paint the ears. When they are dry, overlap the edges of the slits. Glue them together to make curved ears.

16

The mask

4 Paint both sides of the mask, giving the wolf beady eyes and a black nose. Glue on the ears.

5 Paint newspaper gray or silver. When it is dry, tear it into strips. Glue them onto the wolf's head.

6 Cut a strip of thin cardboard to fit around your head. Tape the ends together. Cut another strip to fit over your head. Tape the strips together to make a crown.

7 Glue or tape the wolf's head onto the crown. Glue the tips of the nose together.

Now frighten someone!

GRRRR

Mighty monsters

Monster masks are designed to be scary. Mask makers use strong colors, strange features, and weird expressions to make monsters look terrifying.

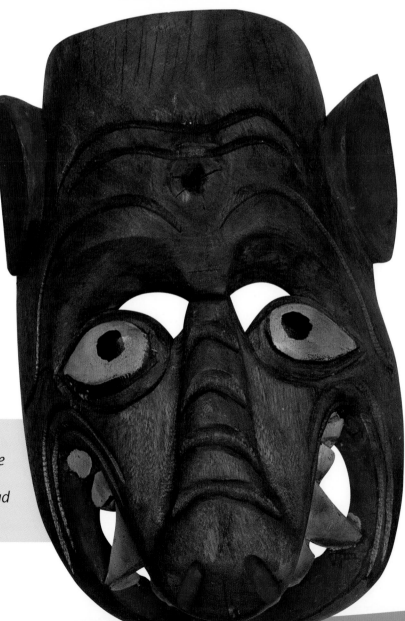

✿ Painted in only a few bold colors and strong, well-defined shapes, this Japanese monster mask has a very menacing look.

Look closer

This monster's features have been enlarged to make it look frightening. It has:

- fat, red ears
- deep frown lines
- huge, bulging eyes
- a wide, open mouth
- sharp tusks
- a very long nose with red nostrils.

✿ The deep grooves on this Mexican wooden mask help define the shape of the mouth and eyes. The lines on the nose and forehead add extra expression.

Lots of different details have been combined to make this monster appear strange. It has:

- the antlers of a deer
- a twisted tongue
- big, hairy eyebrows
- lizards on its cheeks
- a spider on its nose.

🌼 *Mexican painted clay masks like these two are hung on walls of homes to scare away evil spirits. They are fired (baked hard) in a kiln (very hot oven) before being painted.*

Look closer

To give this monster a really threatening and unfriendly expression, it has:

- a spotted face
- sharp horns
- a big, red stuck-out tongue
- staring eyes and big ears.

Making a monster mask

1 Press and stretch a lump of modeling clay on a wooden board, until it is soft and easy to work with.

Model the shape of a monster's head and a pair of ears.

2 Use extra clay to model eyes, a nose, and a mouth, and any other features, such as horns. Attach them to the face, smoothing over the joins.

3 Add extra details, such as a tongue, nostrils, hair, eyebrows, and pupils for the eyes. Leave the clay to dry.

Tip: Use a pencil tip to give a bumpy texture to the ears.

4 Paint your monster in vivid, contrasting colors. Add spots, stripes, and other patterns.

Curious creatures

The makers of these masks focused on the main features of each creature. The elephant's ears were made separately and joined to the face with string. The snake twists and turns to fit a face. The birds have big beaks that stick out from the face.

Look closer

Notice how patterns help bring out the shapes of the elephant's features.

- The long trunk has forked lines along its length.
- The eyes are circled and spotted.
- The forehead has colored stripes.

At festivals in India, real elephants are often painted with markings similar to those on this Indian papier-mâché mask.

- The eyes have been placed on the side of these masks, instead of the front, making them look more birdlike.
- Notice how the shape and angle of the birds' beaks give them very different expressions.

Stands sell fun masks, like these bird heads, during festivals in Mexico.

Chinese snake mask.

Look closer

- The head of this snake sits on the mask-wearer's nose.
- Coils frame the eyes.
- The tail curls over the forehead, looking like a lock of hair.

This mask comes from Java, part of Indonesia. It is the head of Garuda, a mythical creature who has the beak, wings, and feet of a bird, and the arms and body of a man. His crown shows that he is king of the birds.

Making a bird mask

- a large plastic bowl ● plastic wrap ● newspaper ● magazines ● white glue ● adhesive tape ● paints ● paintbrush ● colored cardboard ● scissors ● hole punch ● round elastic

1 Cover a bowl with plastc wrap, making sure it overlaps the rim. Cover the sides (but *not* the bottom) of the bowl with papier-mâché (see page 31). Leave it to dry.

2 Cut a circle (the size of a dinner plate) from several layers of newspaper. Cut a slit to the center of the circle. Curve the paper into a cone. Tape it inside and out.

Circle

Cone

3 Fit the cone halfway over the hole in the mask to make a beak. Fix it onto the mask with more layers of papier-mâché. Let it dry.

4 Paint the mask
and leave it to dry.

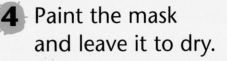

Cardboard
feathers

5 Cut out colored cardboard
feathers. Bend up the flat
end of each one.

Glue the bent ends onto
the mask. Overlap each
feather and make sure they
all stand up.

6 Paint eyes on
the mask. Fit
elastic onto the
sides, to hold
the mask onto
your head (see
page 30).

Performing players

Actors sometimes wear masks to perform dance dramas. The audience usually knows the story and recognizes the characters from their masks.

✺ In parts of Indonesia, actors perform the Ramayana, a Hindu epic, which tells the story of how Rama rescues his wife Sita, who has been kidnapped by Ravanna, the evil, ten-headed demon king. This painted wooden mask represents Ravanna.

✺ This is the mask of Hanuman, the monkey king, who, with his army, helps defeat Ravanna, the demon king.

Look closer

The color and the facial expressions show what characters in dramas are like.

- Good characters, like Hanuman, are white. Hanuman's face is strong and warlike.

- Bad characters, like Ravanna, have bulging eyes and fangs. The crown shows Ravanna is a king.

☼ *Young men in Michocoan, Mexico, perform a funny dance pretending to be little old men. They put on masks of old men and hobble around with walking sticks. All of a sudden, they break into a lively dance, clacking their wooden shoes in time to fast music.*

Look closer

- The devil is painted red and black—colors that often portray evil.

- He has long, sharp horns.

- The pointy tips of his black mustache and beard echo the shape of the horns.

☼ *Lucifer, the devil, is a masked character in a Mexican Christmas play, called the Pastorela. This tells the story of the shepherds' journey to visit the newborn Jesus, and how they overcome the temptations that the devil offers them on their way.*

Making a dramatic mask

The head

You will need

- an empty cereal box ● scissors
- thin cardboard ● a pencil
- paints and a paintbrush
- two empty yogurt cartons
- a cardboard tube ● white glue

1 Unfold one of the short ends of a large cereal box. Cut one of the long sides in half. Open out the two sides, as shown.

2 Cut two small eye holes in the center of the opposite, uncut long side of the box.

3 Turn the box over and paint it.

The teeth

4 Cut two rows of large card teeth, like this.

The ears

5 Cut two big card ears. Bend over a flap of ½in (1cm) on the straight edges. Paint them.

The nose

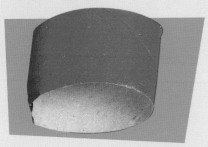

7 Cut a small piece off of a cardboard tube. Paint it the same color as the box.

8 Paint the inside black. Squash and glue the cylinder to make a nose.

The eyes

6 Paint two yogurt cartons exactly the same color. Paint on eyes.

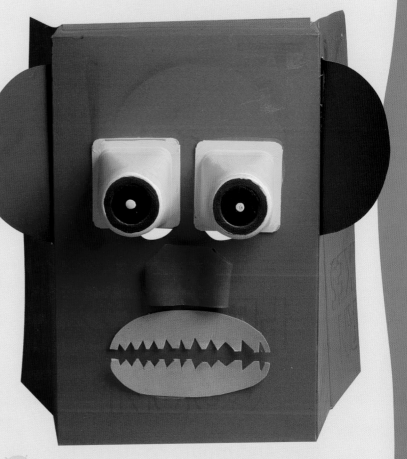

9 Glue the eyes just above the eye holes. Glue the ears, nose, and teeth in place. Attach some elastic to the sides (see page 30).

Handy hints

Marking a mask

1 Hold a paper plate up to your face. Ask someone to mark where your eyes, nose, and mouth are. The eyes should be about 2¼in (6cm) apart.

2 Pierce the center of the eyes and mouth to start cutting them out. Only cut around the sides and bottom of the nose, making a flap.

Putting on a mask

1 Using a hole punch, make a hole on either side of the mask, about the same level as the eye holes.

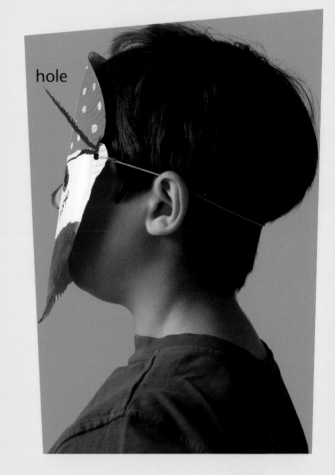

hole

2 Cut some round elastic, long enough to fit around the back of your head.

3 Thread one end through each hole and knot it in place.

Making papier-mâché

1 Tear newspaper into small pieces and put them into a pile. Tear pages from a color magazine into similar pieces. Keep these in a separate pile.

newspaper pieces

magazine pieces

2 Mix white glue with the same amount of water in a bowl or jug. Dip in the newspaper pieces and overlap them onto your mold.

3 Once your mold is covered with a layer of newspaper strips, cover it with a layer of magazine pieces. This way you can tell when you have finished each layer of papier-mâché. Alternate newspaper and magazine strips for seven layers.

Glossary

carnival an outdoor celebration where people dress up and move along in a parade, singing and dancing

disguise to hide who you are

exaggerate to make something seem bigger or more important than it really is

fangs the long, sharp teeth of fierce animals and snakes

muzzle the front part, including the nose and mouth, of an animal's face

spirit a supernatural being

Index